Bingo!

Bingo!

The Secret to Scrabble Success

Michael Betzold

iUniverse, Inc.
New York   Bloomington

Bingo!
The Secret to Scrabble Success

Copyright © 2010 Michael Betzold

Cover photo by Kate Whitney

iUniverse books may be ordered through booksellers or by contacting:

iUniverse
1663 Liberty Drive
Bloomington, IN 47403
www.iuniverse.com
1-800-Authors (1-800-288-4677)

ISBN: 978-1-4502-3440-5 (pbk)
ISBN: 978-1-4502-3441-2 (ebk)

Printed in the United States of America

iUniverse rev. date: 6/2/2010

Contents

PREFACE
The Test of Time

Scrabble is a trademarked game made by Hasbro Inc in Canada, and in the rest of the world by J.W Spear & Sons of England. This book is not authorized by the manufacturers of Scrabble. It is my own take on the game, formed from years of casually competitive play and what I've learned from many skilled and imaginative opponents.

This book is not for experts or word freaks. It is intended to teach casual players familiar with the game of Scrabble the basics of "bingo strategy"—the key to how ordinary players become more advanced— along with a few other tactics. It is shaped by experiences I have had playing the game and teaching my version of bingo strategy in adult education classes and to various friends.

To benefit from this book you need not be a word whiz or a game genius. All you need is an enthusiasm for Scrabble and a willingness to alter your old habits and learn new tricks. If you read this book and practice its suggestions, I guarantee you will greatly increase your enjoyment of Scrabble as well as your game scores. You will add 50, 100, or more points to your average score. And by grasping a whole new level of play you can learn to expand the game from something enjoyable to something fascinating. I will open a magical door for you.

Only a very few games survive the ultimate test of time. When unemployed architect Alfred Butts created the game he first called "Criss Cross Words" in the 1930s, his inspiration and hard work combined to produce a near-perfect pleasure. Unaided by computer analysis, he catalogued the frequency of letters in stories in the *New York Times* to determine the distribution of his 100 game tiles. Modeling his game board on the common fifteen-by-fifteen crossword puzzle grid, Butts placed the bonus squares in exactly the right spots and devised the point values for each letter. Luckily, he also included two blanks and the 50-point bonus for playing seven letters in a single turn.

The genius of Butts is now clearer than ever. As many thousands of new words have been allowed in the Scrabble dictionary, and as new generations of players have discovered new tactics and possibilities, the game remains a fascinating challenge.

It's a bit like the story of baseball—another game I am extremely fond of. In 1848, when Alexander Cartwright, a volunteer fireman in Manhattan, laid out his Knickerbocker Club's baseball diamond on the Elysian Fields in Hoboken, New Jersey, he set the bases 90 feet apart, a distance that proved exactly right and remains so more than 160 years later.

So, too, Butts's seven letters per player per turn, his 100 well-distributed tiles with their range of point values, his board with the cleverly placed bonus squares, and his "bingo" reward still work together to create magic. As with baseball, Scrabble today has stronger players, knowledge of the game keeps advancing, each game remains a fresh challenge, and new situations are always unfolding—yet the basic scheme endures and the game world the originator created remains a thing of beauty.

I've been playing Scrabble since I was a kid. I remember taking on my father after 6:30 a.m. Mass every Sunday morning during my preteen and teen years—and beating him the majority of the time. In the late 1970s, an acquaintance showed me the basics of the same "bingo strategy" I explain in this book. Armed with my new knowledge, I played at a few local clubs in the early 1980s, when tournament Scrabble was just beginning.

However, since I didn't care to spend my spare hours memorizing lists of obscure words, I stopped just short of fanaticism. Today, I am not a regular tournament player—just a good competitive player who plays for fun once a week at a local club in Ann Arbor, Michigan. There, I have learned lots of new words and tricks, but the basic strategy that transformed my game more than thirty years ago continues to be the framework I use. And that's what I want to teach you.

CHAPTER 1
Rules and Fundamentals

I'M NOT GOING TO TEACH you how to play Scrabble. I'm assuming you already know how, or you wouldn't have picked up this book. You've played it at the dining room table with Grandma, your spouse, your kids, or maybe online with distant friends and new acquaintances. You know the basic rules.

Over the years, however, families and friends have adopted their own variations. Some people allow the blank to be "recycled" after it's played by substituting a tile for the letter it was designated to be. Others allow looking up words in the dictionary beforehand.

Many players aren't even aware of all the official rules—most notably, the rule about being able to use a turn to trade in letters.

Obviously, you can play the game however you choose. But let's get on the same page here. Throughout this book, I'm going to assume we're playing by the rules we use at our club—the official game rules that can be found in every game box, plus a few additional ones commonly used at tournaments. This chapter will clarify those rules.

It Takes Two to Tangle

Scrabble can be played by two, three, or four people, but it's much more competitive and enjoyable as a two-person game. From this point forward, I am assuming that you're playing against only one opponent. If you play with three or four, it's a fun social game—but you no longer have control over your strategy, so using the "bingo strategy" won't pay off consistently. In this book, you will learn the strategy for playing a two-person game.

Starting the Game

To see who goes first, each player draws a single tile from the pool. The player who draws the letter closer to "A" goes first (the blank beats any tile). If both draw the same letter, each must draw again until the tie is broken.

Return the tiles drawn to the pool. The player who goes first draws seven fresh tiles and then the other player draws hers.

Blanks

Each of the two blank tiles may be used as any letter. When playing a blank, you must announce what letter it represents. It remains that letter for the rest of the game and stays on the board.

The point value of the blank is zero.

Bingos

If you play all seven tiles on a single turn, it's a "bingo," and you are awarded 50 bonus points in addition to the score for the play. After you digest this book, you will be getting at least one bingo bonus in nearly every game you play!

You cannot get a bingo bonus if you play fewer than seven tiles.

Exchanging Tiles

Instead of making a word, you may pass your turn. If you pass, you can keep all your tiles, or you can exchange any number of tiles. To trade in letters, place the ones you are discarding facedown. Draw the same number of tiles from the pool, and then put the discarded tiles back. This ends your turn.

You cannot use your turn to exchange letters if there are fewer than seven tiles left in the pool. However, you can still pass your turn if you want.

Taking Too Many Tiles

There is nothing in the rules about what to do if your opponent draws too many tiles. Since this is a common error, the North American Scrabble Players Association has devised a rule that works very well—and will make you more careful in drawing the right number of tiles the next time! If you end up with eight letters in a rack, your opponent draws three of them without looking at any, turns them face-up on the table, and then selects one of the three to put back in the pool.

The Dictionary

Since 1979, Scrabble players have relied on the Merriam-Webster *Official Scrabble Players Dictionary* to be the authority on allowable words. In 2005, Hasbro published the dictionary's Fourth Edition, which incorporated about 4,000 new words, including the two-letter powerhouses "qi" and "za," which changed the game dramatically.

A funny thing happened on the way to the Fourth. After the publication of the official Second Edition of the Scrabble dictionary in 1990, protesters offended by the inclusion of the word "jew" as a verb—and other slurs and obscenities—mounted a campaign that resulted in a cleaned-up "family" version, the Third Edition. Dozens of words were purged, and most of them still do not appear in the Fourth.

The scrubbing of the dictionary drew howls of protest from members of the North American Scrabble Players Association (NASPA), who threatened a boycott over the removal of words they depended on using The solution was the publication of the *Official Tournament and Club Word List* (OWL), also published by Merriam-Webster, which includes all the banned words. This dictionary, available through the NASPA, contains no definitions; it includes all eight- and nine-letter words and their derivatives.

At our club, we allow the expurgated words and rely on the OWL as our authority. You can choose to rely on the Fourth, or the OWL, or supplement the Fourth with this handy list of the censored words at http://home.teleport.com/~stevena/scrabble/expurg.html.

In other countries, including England, a different word list called SOWPODS is the authority; it includes all the OWL words, plus British words included in the *Collins English Dictionary*. If you play online, you might be using SOWPODS, depending on the site.

Challenging

Whatever choice you make about the "naughty" words, it's important to agree on an authoritative dictionary to settle challenges. In club play, you aren't allowed to look up words in the dictionary beforehand.

Any play may be challenged. If you are considering a challenge, say "hold" or "wait a minute" before your opponent draws new tiles. You can think for a little bit before you decide whether to challenge. If a challenge is lodged, any and all words made on the play are subject to the challenge.

The challenger—or a neutral third party—looks up the word or words in the official dictionary. If any of the words played is no good, the play is removed from the board, and the player being challenged puts the tiles back in her rack and loses her turn.

However, if all the words played are in the dictionary, the challenger lose her turn. The play stands, and the challenged player draws replacement tiles, and gets to play again. The challenger loses a turn. (Note: you shouldn't say anything about the words challenged except whether the challenge is good or not.)

Ending the Game

A game ends when there are no tiles left in the bag, and one player plays the last of her letters. The value of the opponents' unplayed tiles is doubled and added to the score of the player who goes out.

A game also ends if there are six consecutive passes—turns where no tiles are played. Sometimes there are tiles remaining, but they cannot be played. Or one of the players may choose to pass at the end rather than play a letter that allows the opponent to play. When the game ends this way, the value of each player's remaining tiles is deducted from her score.

CHAPTER 2
Your Fate Is in Your Hands

MOST GAMES ARE A COMBINATION of skill and luck in different measures. Chess quickly comes to mind as a game that's all skill and Bingo as a game that is all luck.

If a game is all skill, you have complete control over what happens. Everybody starts each chess game with the same pieces in the same places, and there is no element of the game that involves chance.

In games of pure chance, you have no control over what happens. Sure, it takes some attention to play several games of Bingo at once, but you have no influence over the numbers that are drawn.

Some people like skill games, and some people like luck games. Most people enjoy games that combine skill and chance. Almost all card, dice, and board games have some combination of chance and skill.

If you've played Scrabble casually, you probably believe that winning involves two things: vocabulary skills and good luck. Allow me to convince you otherwise. While both vocabulary and luck do play important roles, winning at Scrabble depends quite heavily on using a winning strategy. This book is dedicated to teaching that strategy.

This book is not going to make you luckier, and it is not aimed at increasing your vocabulary. Instead, it will break down for you in easy steps the strategy that Scrabble champions use to win games. You can use that strategy regardless of the size of your vocabulary, and it will diminish the role of luck.

What letters you draw on any turn or in any game will continue to be something you can't totally control—that's the inevitable role of chance in Scrabble. However, you *can* employ strategies that will

5

maximize your chances of getting the letters you need to win each game. Over the long run, my strategy will give you the tools to win without relying on chance.

Here's what's actually involved in playing great Scrabble and how this book will help you with each component:

(1) Luck—the letters you draw. This book will help you learn how to reduce greatly the role that luck plays in your game by giving you tips on how to improve your chances of getting more useful letters and getting rid of difficult ones.

(2) Anagramming—the ability to form words from the letters you have. This skill depends on the number of words you know and on your skill at finding them in the letters you select plus those already on the board. A large vocabulary obviously helps. But a large everyday vocabulary is not the same as a large Scrabble vocabulary. There are thousands of "Scrabble words" that are rarely if ever used outside of the game.

I'll tell you later what methods you can use to improve your Scrabble vocabulary and tips on honing your anagramming skills. It's largely a matter of practice, so it's mostly up to you.

(3) Game strategy. You already know that the ability to see how to place words on the board for a maximum score on each turn is a key to winning games. Scrabble is often accurately described as a math game and a board game as well as a word game. You might define a good Scrabble player as someone who can find and make words that place high-value tiles in point-producing combinations, using the board's bonus squares. Later in the book, I'm going to show you some keys to getting better at the crucial skill of finding the places to score higher.

But first I'm going to blow your mind. There's an even more powerful way to play than the point-producing methods you're familiar with. I'm going to show you a whole new way to play Scrabble. This strategy will instantly elevate your game to a new level.

The curious thing about this strategy is that at first it will seem like you're being told to play the opposite of the way you've been playing all your life.

The strategy is focused on making bingos—using all your letters on a single turn. To some of you, this may seem like something that just happens once in a blue moon. But if you read this book and practice what I teach you, it will become a routine occurrence for you, even if you don't have a huge vocabulary or expert anagramming skills.

The bingo strategy is an open secret that tens of thousands of the best Scrabble players know. The strategy has been around for at least thirty years. Yet most casual Scrabble players have never learned it.

I guarantee it will work and vastly increase your interest and pleasure in playing the game.

CHAPTER 3
Bingo Basics

Let's turn our attention now to the play that's going to transform your Scrabble experience – the bingo—starting with the basics.

What is a bingo? It's any play where you use all seven letters in your rack.

Why is making bingos so important? If you make a bingo, you get all the points for your word plus a 50-point bonus. Usually you will make a total of 60 to 90 points and sometimes much more by playing a bingo.

Don't you have to be incredibly good or incredibly lucky to make a bingo? Neither. If you are a fairly good player and you follow the strategy I outline in this book, you should be able to make an average of one bingo a game. If you are a really good player, you should eventually average about two bingos a game, as I do. That's how your score is going to increase considerably.

How do I do that? So far, you've probably just waited for bingos to fall into your lap, but that happens rarely. If you follow my advice and learn how to *manage your rack* to increase your chances of getting *bingo letters,* bingos will occur more often. By following some simple steps, you can take more control of the game and get more bingos and 50-point bonuses. You can stop waiting for a lucky day and make your own luck.

CHAPTER 4
Old Lovers

THE FIRST STEP TOWARD GETTING more bingos more often is to begin to recognize good *bingo letters*.

Let's start by applying some common sense. The letters that Alfred Butts made the most common in the 100-letter Scrabble pool are the ones that he found most frequently in English words in his examination of the *New York Times*. To these letters he assigned the lowest point values, because they are the easiest to form words with. At the other extreme, Butts gave the highest point values to the letters that are the least common in English words.

If you've been playing Scrabble casually for years, you've probably long been enamored with the large point values of the Q and Z (10 each) and the J and X (8 each). You can't wait to get one of these letters, and you tend to hang onto them until you find a great place to play them. Most people seek to play these high-value letters on high-value bonus squares, the double or triple letter scores and the double or triple word scores, and they are willing to wait several turns until they get that opportunity.

It's true that you can score lots of points by using these "big" tiles in combination with bonus squares on the board, and you should continue to try to do so. Quite often, you can make 25, 30, 40, and occasionally lots more points with these monster tiles. But that's a lot less than you score by playing a bingo, with its automatic 50-point bonus.

If you're so much in love with the J, Q, X, and Z that you hold onto these letters, turn after turn, until you can find a way to play them for big points, you're clinging to a losing strategy. If you want to make bingos, these letters must no longer be your sweethearts. Because they

9

occur so rarely in long words, they are huge impediments to making bingos, and you should *get rid of them as soon as possible!* You should play them for whatever points you can get, or trade them in immediately for new, more productive letters!

Generally speaking, the more points a letter is assigned, the less commonly it appears in words, and the harder it is to use it to make bingos. So you want to get rid of such letters as quickly as you can, especially at the beginning of the game, when the board is usually wide open for bingos.

At first, to dump your old sweethearts like hot potatoes will feel counterintuitive to some of you. But soon you will see why you must do so.

CHAPTER 5
New Sweethearts

It's TIME TO MEET YOUR new favorite letters. They're not as flashy as those high scorers like Q and Z, but they're productive workers who can join forces to make a big bang.

Let's start by looking at the frequency of letters in the Scrabble pool.

Scrabble Letter Values And Frequency

Consonants	Value	Frequency
Q, Z	10	1
J, X	8	1
K	5	1
F, H, V, W, Y	4	2
B, C, M, P	3	2
G	2	3
D	2	4
L, S	1	4
N, R, T	1	6
Vowels		
U	1	4
O	1	8
A, I	1	9
E	1	12
Blank	0	2

The more common a letter is, the better it is for making bingos. So the best vowel to have is an E, followed by the A and the I, and then the O. The U is not nearly as good.

Among consonants, the N, R, and T are the clear favorites.

The S is the most valuable letter in helping you make a bingo. Not only is the S a common letter in many words, it is the primary way English makes nouns into plurals and verbs into the form used with singular subjects—so having it often provides you with an easy way to turn a six-letter word into a seven-letter bingo. And it is also the easiest letter to use to "hook" a bingo onto the board by adding to a word that's already been played.

The only tile more valuable than the S is the blank. It should be obvious why. The blank has no point value, but you can use it as any letter. *You should almost always try to use the blank to make a bingo.*

Here's an easy way to remember the most valuable tiles for making bingos, in this order:

The blank
The S
The letters in RETAIN
The letters in GOLD

CHAPTER 6
Watching the Pretty Leaves

NOW THAT YOU KNOW WHAT letters you want to romance, how do you attract and keep them?

Answer: You manage your rack.

"Managing your rack" means you take more control over what letters you are going to work with on your *next* turn.

You can maximize your chances of making bingos by keeping bingo-friendly tiles in your rack to work with the new letters you draw on each turn. This is the key way your game should change—by following this rule: *On each turn, pay as much attention to what you leave in your rack as to what you play on the board.*

Most casual players try to make the most points on every turn. But you don't win a Scrabble *game* this way. The player with the most points at the end is the winner. And making bingos sometimes requires taking several turns to accumulate the right combination of bingo-friendly letters in your rack. To do so, you might sometimes take fewer points on a turn to give you the best chance to score a blockbuster bingo later. Would you rather make 25, 15, and 20 points on consecutive turns—or 10, 15, and then 80 points? The bingo strategy I'm teaching will often give you that total of 105 points rather than the 60 points you'd get with your old tactics.

If you make the most points you can on a turn but leave yourself with a lousy rack (say, I, I, U, V), you're probably going to endure two or more really awful turns before you can possibly make a bingo. So balance your desire for accumulating quick points with this new strategy of husbanding bingo letters for success over the long haul.

To make this strategy of managing your rack work to its utmost, it is crucial to understand what constitutes *a good leave*. A good leave follows these three main rules:

1. Keep good bingo letters in your rack.

Dump your old lovers and hang onto your new sweethearts. The blank should almost always be saved for a bingo. Don't waste it to score a mere 20 or 30 points (except at the end of the game). Also, the S should usually be saved for a bingo, especially early in the game. Otherwise, try to *retain the letters in RETAIN* and, finally, *go for the GOLD*.

2. Try to keep a balance of vowels and consonants.

Most seven-letter words are going to require at least two vowels and at least two consonants. If you've got nothing but one or the other, your chances of making an English word diminish—even though you might come up with something great in Hawaiian or Czech. So, whenever possible, aim for a leave that is a nice mix of vowels and consonants.

3. Avoid duplication (more than one of the same letter).

It's harder to make bingos if you have two or three of the same letter, even the S, so get rid of your duplicates. The only exception to this advice is the E—lots of seven-letter words have two Es, and quite a few even have three.

When playing a word, always look at the letters that will be left in your rack after your play. Remember the three elements you are striving for—keeping bingo letters, keeping a balance of vowels and consonants, and avoiding duplication.

Of course, it's not always a perfect world. In practice, it's often impossible to achieve all three aspects of a good leave at the same time. But try to get as close as you can. Start learning to judge what a good leave is, and start striving to see as many pretty leaves as possible.

QUIZ ONE: GOOD LEAVES

Let's take a little quiz to test your understanding of what a good leave is. *For each of these racks, what letters would you ideally like to play?* (*Denotes the blank.)

Q1. A A M M O O T

Q2. A E N R T W Y

Q3. O P R S S T U

Q4. D E G I N V X

Q5. A I L N O Q U

Q6. H I L M N O R

Q7. C E E I I S *

Q8. A E I I S T U

Q9. B E H J I S *

The answers are on the next page, in Chapter 7.

CHAPTER 7
Rack and Roll

TRYING TO KEEP GOOD BINGO letters in your rack is the key tactic in getting more bingos. In practice, however, it's usually a balancing act.

In Quiz One, these are the letters you should try to play to leave the optimal rack for a future bingo:

Q1. A, M, O
Q2. W, Y
Q3. P, S, U
Q4. V, X
Q5. O, Q, U
Q6. H, M
Q7. C, E, I
Q8. I, U
Q9. B, H, J

You can easily see, however, that playing actual words with the letters that you want to get rid of is not always possible.

In #1, MOA is a word you can play. In #3, you could play SOUP. In #6, HM is an acceptable Scrabble word. In most of the others, you might be able to combine the letters you want to play with a letter on the board.

But how can you play only the letters B, H, and J in question 9? You can't. The ideal is rarely attainable. But it's still important to identify the letters you don't want as a first step *before* you consider a play.

On each play, *start* by deciding which letters you ideally would like to get rid of and which you'd like to keep. Then look for the best play that eliminates your unwanted letters. Balance your desire to score lots of points immediately with keeping a favorable rack for bingos.

Sometimes, you won't keep the best leave because you can make a much higher-scoring play by using some of the bingo-friendly letters. But if you have two different words you could play for about the same amount of points, choose the one that allows you the best leave.

Sometimes you should even play a word for fewer points if so doing leaves you with an appreciably better rack than an alternative, higher-scoring play.

How does this work in practice? Let's look at a couple of examples.

Let's say you are starting the game and your rack is:

A, B, I, N, T, U, Y

Start by asking which letters you want to keep. The ideal leave is A, I, N, T—four of the letters in RETAIN, no duplicate letters, and a balance of vowels and consonants. The decision should be easy. You should play BUY, getting rid of all your less valuable bingo letters.

But let's say your initial rack is:

I, O, R, S, T, V, W

The letters you want to keep are I, O, R, S, T. You could play VOW for 18 points and leave yourself with a good though slightly unbalanced rack. There is a higher-scoring play: WRIST for 24 points. But making WRIST squanders your valuable S and leaves you with O and V—a bad leave. The six extra points are definitely not worth it in the long run, so sacrifice them to keep the good bingo letters. Don't waste the S to get a few points.

Remember: the way to win is not to get the most points every turn. It's to maximize your chances for getting bingos, so that you can get the highest score for the entire game.

CHAPTER 8
Shocking Trade News

PLAYING SCRABBLE, YOU'LL OFTEN HEAR these complaints: "I have a terrible rack. ... My letters are awful. ... I have the worst luck. ... I just never get any good letters."

You've already learned how to improve your chances of getting good racks by making good leaves. Using that skill will somewhat reduce the number of truly awful racks you will have. But there will still be times when you get stuck with racks like:

A I I I I U Y

or

B C D J V V W

If you keep trying to play words with racks like these, it can take several turns to recover. But what choice do you have?

Actually, you don't have to put up with such bad racks. On any turn you can pass instead of playing. And when you pass, you can trade in any number of letters—none, some, or all of what's in your rack. (Remember, though, you can't exchange letters if there are fewer than seven letters remaining in the pool.)

Exchanging tiles is not just a rare desperation move. In fact, it should become a regular practice for you. It's a crucial tactic in building good bingo racks, and good players often exchange letters once or twice a game—and sometimes even more often. Keep this in mind:

If you cannot make a decent play that gets you a great score immediately or that leaves you with a good rack for bingos, consider trading in some or all of your letters.

This is the answer to what you might do with question #9 in Quiz

One at the end of Chapter 6. You cannot play the B, H, and J, so you might exchange them.

In what circumstances should you consider exchanging letters?

1. Your hand is hopelessly unbalanced. You have six or seven vowels or consonants and no hope of playing most of them on one turn. No matter what you do, you will leave yourself with an unbalanced rack. You can either be stuck with low-scoring plays and bad leaves for several turns, or you can give yourself a much better chance to get a bingo.

2: You have no high-scoring play, and the best options will leave you with a bad rack—bad bingo tiles, an unbalanced rack, or duplication of letters. Example: You have

C C F L M O U

You can't play more than three of these letters unless you play FOUL, and that leaves you with the awful rack of C, C, M. Let's say you can make 11 points by playing FOUL with the F on a double-letter score. You are better off trading in all your letters. Sacrificing the eleven points greatly increases your chances of getting a bingo on the next turn or turns.

Exchanging letters, especially early in the game, gives you the best chance to draw a blank or an S. The more letters you trade, the better chance you have of getting these extremely valuable tiles. Early in the game it is usually right to *trade in all your letters.* Or you can keep a balanced selection of any of the letters in RETAIN.

An exception is if your rack is extremely unbalanced. Remember that you choose your replacement letters *before* you put the relinquished letters back in the bag. Some players keep a vowel (preferably an E) if their rack is all vowels and keep a good consonant (an N, R, or T) if their rack is all consonants. That's because the rack you are just turning in has caused there to be an imbalance of vowels and consonants remaining in the bag. You're more likely to draw vowels if you turn in all consonants, and vice versa. Of course, there is no guarantee of this, but it's a matter of playing the odds.

The same principle applies to playing words as it does to trading. When there are still valuable tiles left in the bag, I try to play as many letters as I can. Making longer words increases your chances of drawing a blank or an S. Early in the game, if my choice is between playing two or three letters and making 20 points and playing six letters for 14 points, I might sacrifice the extra points and play the longer word, especially if the higher-scoring play leaves me with a less desirable rack.

CHAPTER 9
Trade Objections

OF ALL THE ADVICE I give people about Scrabble, the tip given in the last chapter meets the most resistance. Many people are reluctant to use the exchange option. Here are some of the objections I often hear:

I've tried trading in letters, and it doesn't help. The ones I get back are worse. Of course, occasionally this *does* happen: you make a trade, and your new rack is no better. There is no guarantee that any particular trade is going to improve your rack. But over the long run more frequent trading will pay off. Most of the time you will get a better rack with one or more good bingo letters, and often you will draw an S or a blank.

Don't abandon a strategy just because it doesn't pay off every single time. Sometimes you even have to pass twice in a row—perhaps the first time you get an S or a blank, but the rest of your letters are terrible. You are trying to build toward a bingo, just as you do by managing your rack, and you won't always hit pay dirt instantly.

I can't waste my turn and not score any points. It's true that you score nothing when you pass a turn. But how many turns of scoring 12 or 15 points equals one turn of scoring 70 or 75 points? Remember, the whole point of this strategy is to make bingos.

The other objections I hear to not exchanging letters are less rational. You might think it's somehow "cheating" or unfair not to play the hand you're dealt. Well, then, you'll have to live with your bad luck. *Perhaps you'd rather whine about your bad luck than try to change it.* "I got such bad letters!" is always a good excuse for losing.

If you add the judicious use of the exchange rule to your arsenal of tactics, I guarantee you will see an immediate improvement in your scores. And you'll have more fun. Instead of passively accepting your fate, you'll be taking positive action to change your luck. And that's what the bingo strategy is all about.

CHAPTER 10
Trade Embargoes

IF YOU HAVE A TRULY unplayable rack, you should almost always exchange your tiles. But there are some times when it's better *not* to exchange your tiles.

When you can make a decent scoring play even if it leaves you a bad rack. There's no hard-and-fast definition of how much you need to score to invoke this rule. It depends on the stage of the game, the ability of your opponent, and the looks of the board. But most players wouldn't pass up 20, 25, or more points at any time in the game.

When there is nothing left in the bag worth trying to get—all the Ss and both blanks are gone. In this situation, it's probably best to work with what you have—unless what you have is truly impossible.

When there's no place on the board to make a bingo. Just getting a bingo in your rack does not mean you can play one (see Chapter 11, "Finding Your Bingos a Home."). If there are no possible places you can play a seven- or eight-letter word, you should abandon your all-out quest for a bingo, at least temporarily.

If you have a big lead late in the game. Instead of risking a comeback by your opponent, it's usually better to just keep adding points to your score by making the best play you can.

QUIZ TWO: INITIAL PLAY

I've given you a lot to digest, and the best way to learn it is to practice it. Let's take a break now and start applying what we've learned.

You are making the first play of the game. What should you do? Play what word? Or trade in what letters? Answers are on page 50.

* Denotes a blank

Your rack	Your play
1. A A E G M N T	_____
2. B C M P W V Y	_____
3. D R S S T U *	_____
4. D D R S S U *	_____
5. D N O S U Y Z	_____
6. A E F G H H I	_____
7. A B C E S V V	_____
8. D O O O O O V	_____

CHAPTER 11
Finding Your Bingos a Home

Now THAT YOU HAVE LEARNED all the strategies for maximizing your chances of getting prime bingo letters, you have diminished the role of luck. That's half the battle. Now you have to turn those promising letters into actual bingos that you can play on the board.

It's not a bingo until you can get it down on the board. Forming a seven-letter word in your rack doesn't get you the 50-point bonus. So, before you even try to find a bingo in your rack, examine the board and look for places to play one.

There are two ways to play bingos.

Hooks: "Hook" is the term for attaching your entire word to an existing word. The easiest way to do this is with an S, which is one reason S is such a valuable letter. You can often add an S to an existing word.

At other times you can hook a letter other than S onto a word to make a bingo. For instance, if the word "EAR" is on the board you can put a B, D, F, G, H, N, P, R, S, T or W in front of it, or an L, N, or S after it. Always look for these opportunities.

More frequently, though, you will hook your bingo onto the board by making a two-letter word or words. *To help you in this task, it is imperative to learn all the officially acceptable two-letter Scrabble words.*

It's easy to get a list of the two-letter words. But my list on the next page organizes them into words you probably already know and words you might not know.

TWO-LETTER WORD LIST

Common Words		Uncommon Words	
AD	LA	AA	MU
AH	LO	AB	NA
AM	MA	AE	NE
AN	ME	AG	NU
AS	MI	AI	OD
AT	MY	AL	OE
AX	NO	AR	OI
BE	OF	AW	OM
BI	OH	AY	OP
BY	ON	BA	OS
DO	OR	BO	OW
EL	OX	DE	OY
EM	PA	ED	PE
EN	PI	EF	QI
EX	RE	EH	SH
FA	SO	ER	SI
GO	TI	ES	TA
HA	TO	ET	UH
HE	UP	FE	UM
HI	US	HM	UN
HO	WE	JO	UT
ID	YE	KA	WO
IF		KI	XI
IN		LI	XU
IS		MM	YA
IT		MO	YO
		ZA	

Eight-letter words: The other way to bingo is to run all seven letters in your rack through an existing letter on the board. Making an eight-letter word is normally harder than making a seven-letter word. (You can also make longer words, nine or even more letters, by adding onto already played words, but that's rare.)

Hunting Down Bingos

The strategy for managing your rack is crucial to making bingos. But even more important is developing the ability to find the bingos in your rack. This means honing your anagramming skills—the same skills you use for making shorter words.

Carefully examining the board will also limit the bingo possibilities of your holding. You'll start your search by saying to yourself something like: *My word has to start with a D or an E. Or it has to end with a E or a T. Or it has to be an eight-letter word with "G" in it.* If you don't take this initial step, you'll often waste time finding a bingo in your rack that can't be played

Improving the anagramming skills that you need to find bingos is largely a matter of practice. But here are some helpful steps in the hunt for seven-letter words:

Breaking it down: Many bingo words have common prefixes or, even more frequently, *suffixes*. So start your search by placing at the end of your rack the letters that could form one of these suffixes:

-ER, -IER –EST, -IEST (these suffixes that make comparative or superlative adjectives produce lots of acceptable bingos)

ED, -IVE, -AGE, -ION, -IES, -IST, -ATE, -ING

If using suffixes doesn't work, try out some **prefixes** like: RE-, DE-, UN-, OUT-, IN-, PRE- ,CON-, MIS-.

Combining letters: If you are shuffling letters, use your existing knowledge of English to construct plausible syllables made up of reasonable consonant-vowel combinations. It's useless to search by putting the letters "HM" in order next to each other, or the letters "II." Keep trying out different orders, but don't waste time on impossible juxtapositions.

Visualization: Don't give up if you don't get a bingo right away. Some people are good at "seeing" a word right off, but even the best anagrammers sometimes need time. Keep looking.

Memorization: The real experts study lists of frequently found racks and memorize all the bingos that can be made from these combinations. You can find places online to help you with this task (see Appendix). But you don't need to memorize lists of words if you're not planning to play at the tournament level, and if your anagramming skills and vocabulary are good. You can use the bingo strategy without becoming a word freak.

QUIZ THREE: SECOND PLAY OF THE GAME

It's time for another chance to practice.

   The first word has been played, and it's your turn. The letter in bold is on the center square. Many of these words are bingos, so here's a chance to practice hunting them down. * denotes a blank. Answers are on page 51.

WORD ON BOARD	YOUR TILES	YOUR PLAY
1. GIMP**S**	D G I O Q T U	_____
2. RAT**E**	A E I I N R T	_____
3. B**OX**	C C G I I N O	_____
4. **TO**ILING	A E M N O R V	_____
5. LA**DY**	N O P S S S *	_____
6. KUDO**S**	C E I I R S T	_____
7. UN**FIT**	B C E R O U X	_____
8. NEW**T**	E F G I O R *	_____

CHAPTER 12
Talking Your Way through a Turn

YOU'VE NOW LEARNED EVERYTHING YOU need to know about the bingo strategy. Making it work requires some practice. But first, make sure you understand how the strategy gives you a new approach to the game.

To incorporate all you've learned so far, this is the way you should talk to yourself on each turn **before** you play:

Is there a place to play a bingo on the board?

Is there a bingo on my rack that fits somewhere on the board?

If not, what letters in my rack would I ideally like to keep?

How many points can I get and keep those good bingo letters?

How many points can I get with other plays and other leaves?

Which is the best play to help me win the game?

If I can't make enough points and/or leave myself a good rack, should I trade?

If I'm trading, which if any letters should I keep?

CHAPTER 13
The Best Defense Is a Good Offense

SOME PEOPLE NATURALLY PLAY GAMES defensively, while others like to be aggressive. In almost any kind of competition, trying to avoid losing is not the best strategy for winning. It's true that there are times to be cautious, but you can't effectively employ the bingo strategy without going on the offensive.

This means that—all things being equal—you should try to open up the board rather than close it off. That's especially true if you are playing someone who doesn't know the bingo strategy or doesn't execute it well. The more you open up the board—by playing words that extend into new spaces—the more you create favorable spots for bingos.

You won't always have that choice, however, and sometimes your letters dictate a different strategy. But here are some general guidelines that should fit in with your new approach to the game:

Don't be mortified about opening up a triple-word-score possibility. If your best play consistent with leaving yourself a good rack opens up a possible triple word score, don't sweat it. Your bingo strategy should outweigh your fear of presenting a gift to your opponent. After all, sometimes your opponent won't be able to make a high-scoring play on the triple—or won't play in that spot at all, and you can do so on your next turn.

One way to play defense is to keep playing offense. Some players make it their highest priority to block their opponents from using the high-value squares, and they will accept a very small turn score to block off a route to a triple word. That's not a good idea, unless that is consistent with your bingo strategy (meaning that it's one of the best plays you can make to leave yourself with a good rack). Instead of making a low-scoring play to block your opponent from a triple-word score, consider making a higher-scoring play to open up another triple-word or high-scoring spot—or to open up a bingo spot.

Later in the game, your strategy should be dictated by the score. If you are ahead in the game and it looks like your opponent's only chance to beat you is to make a bingo, that's the time to make *closing off bingo spots* (and other high-scoring spots) your priority. This is the time to play defense, but don't forget, continuing to get high scores is crucial.

Conversely, if you need a bingo to catch up, plan your interim plays in a way that opens up more bingo spots or premium value squares, if you can.

CHAPTER 14
Miracle Comebacks

ONE OF THE BEST THINGS about the bingo strategy is that you're rarely out of any game. If you keep leaving yourself in the best position to use all your letters, there's no telling what can happen. The game becomes much more exciting no matter what the score is.

If it's nearing the end of the game and you're 60 or more points behind, don't give up. In this situation, you should pin your hopes on getting a game-changing bingo.

Sometimes you will end the game with a bingo, in which case you can suddenly turn an 80- or 90-point deficit into a victory (after you collect not only the bingo score, but the points from doubling the value of the unused letters in your opponent's rack).

On rare occasions, two bingos at the end of the game can turn a 150-point deficit into a victory. You now have a powerful arsenal in your toolbox, and your opponent must beware.

CHAPTER 15
Suspending the Quest

THE BINGO STRATEGY IS THE right tool to use for most of the game. But it's not meant to replace common sense. There are certain situations when playing for a bingo is futile and you should go back to playing for the most points each turn:

The board will not permit a bingo. Sometimes your game results in a board where there are no seven-letter "lanes" at all, or you are boxed into a couple of corners (an often-seen pattern is a "stairstep" configuration running diagonally along the double word-score bonus squares). If all bingo avenues are hopelessly blocked, look for other ways to score big. Sometimes the board is only temporarily unsuitable for bingos. If this is the case and you have good bingo letters, try to create a spot to play a bingo by playing one, two, or three of your tiles.

It's late in the game, and you have a substantial lead. You should still keep a lookout for bingos, but don't build your entire strategy around so doing. Keep making plays that get you points and maintain your lead, and don't take big risks by taking lower scores or exchanging tiles in the hope of getting a late bingo. Play a little more conservatively with a lead.

The prime bingo letters—both blanks and all the S's—are already played. In a typical expert game, probably about half the bingos involve the use of blanks and another third use an S. Once those letters are gone, your odds of making a bingo decline. You can still try to keep the letters in RETAIN and GOLD and build towards a bingo, but shift your strategy toward making high-point plays rather than banking everything on bingos.

You have high-value tiles and the score is fairly close late in the game.

In this case, you should make a big play with a J, Q, X, or Z, and not worry about what you leave in your rack. In fact, if you can score 20, 25, or more points at just about any point in the game, you should do so as long as you are not sacrificing a blank or an S to make such a play. Near the end, of course, there is another reason to play the high-pointers: you don't want to get stuck with them if your opponent goes out.

CHAPTER 16
Testing Out the Bingo Strategy

You've now learned everything you need to know about the bingo strategy, and that knowledge will transform your game.

It's going to take some practice for you to figure out how to fit these new tactics into the way you play. The best way to learn is by playing regularly, face-to-face or online. You'll see firsthand how the strategy increases your score and your enjoyment of the game. I strongly recommend you play two-person games.

If you apply what you've learned in this book, there is no doubt you will start increasing the number of bingos you get. You will definitely get more bingo letters in your rack, so all you have to do is keep improving your anagramming skills. Then you can find the bingos and play them. Soon bingos will be a regular occurrence in your games rather than a rare event.

You can also practice in solitaire fashion. Set up a game with two racks and try to make the best plays for each "opponent." See how quickly you can turn bad racks into bingos by exchanging letters or playing your poorer bingo letters to build a good rack. Get comfortable with taking the small risks involved in sometimes giving up a few points on a turn to improve your chances of getting a bingo.

CHAPTER 17
Other Ways to Score Big

PLAYING FOR BINGOS IS NOT a substitute for the other skills that are important in Scrabble. It's a very powerful new tool in your arsenal that will increase your scores—but only if you use common sense in combining it with more familiar ways of scoring points.

Besides making bingos, good Scrabble players get high scores by taking full advantage of the opportunities that the bonus squares on the board present.

You already know that the bonus squares, especially used in combination with the high-value tiles, can pump up your scores. You should continue to hunt for these possibilities. Nothing you've learned in this book should deter you from trying to find them. Once in awhile, they'll even score more than a bingo.

Double bonuses

What really boosts the power of the higher-valued letters is exploiting *bonus-square combinations* on the board. Here are the most valuable such places on the board:

A double-letter score in combination with a triple-word score. You can score by placing a high-value tile on the double-letter spot. For example, ZEST with the Z on the double-letter square and the T on a triple-word square nets you 69 points.

A triple-letter score in combination with a double-word score. These opportunities are near the four corners of the board. You can make a five-letter (or longer) word on a double-word score with a high-value tile on the triple-letter square. Example: WOUND with the W on the triple spot for 34 points. A list of five-letter words that begin or end with a high-value tile is available at www.wvscrabble.com/downloads/wordlists/high_5s.pdf.

Double-doubles. Often overlooked are chances to string a word across two double-word squares near the center of the board. A seven-letter will be needed but not necessarily a bingo (you'll need to play only six letters if one is already on the board). By doubling the total letter values of the word twice, this play scores four times the value of the individual letters—and is thus more potent than the more common play on a triple-word score.

Triple-triples. The rarely achieved grand prize of Scrabble is making an eight-letter bingo that stretches across two triple-word scores. To do so, you will need to find a word that goes through an already played letter on an outer row of the board. This play will score in the triple digits—nine times the face value of the word plus the bingo bonus. Always take a look at such an opportunity—one day you will find a word that fits and hit the jackpot.

Hot spots and two-way plays

Good players are always on the lookout for another common way to exploit bonus squares to score big: by placing tiles on bonus squares to create two words at the same time, doubling the value of the letters or words.

You've no doubt hit it big with the X a time or two, since there are so many two-letter words involving X. You've plopped it down on a triple-letter score, making OX and EX at the same time, or XI and XU, and scored 48 points just for the X. With the inclusion of QI and ZA as words, both the Q and Z are now also in the running for this sort of play.

Scrabble stalwarts often use the 2-, 3-, and 4-point tiles (and the 5-point K) on *hot spot* squares in productive combinations. If you place an H on a triple-letter score and it makes a word going in both directions, you score 24 points just for the H alone.

Always look for hot-spot opportunities for two-way plays on any colored squares. To fully exploit these possibilities, you must know all the two-letter words.

Usually such a play involves making a two-letter word or words, but sometimes you can add onto a two-letter word to make a three-letter, or even longer, word. That's why good Scrabble players like to learn what letters can go on the beginning or end of other common words.

Good players frequently make two-way plays that produce multiple words, because they usually yield higher scores. If you are used to making one word per turn, you should change your approach. Even without placing letters on bonus-square hot spots, you can almost always get more points by stringing your tiles alongside an existing word to produce two, three, or more words in one play.

Opening Tip

It's because of the power that double-letter squares have in combination with higher-value tiles that good players have a rule of thumb about the opening play in a game: try to place consonants, rather than vowels, next to the double-letter squares. If you put a vowel next to a double-letter square, it's much more likely your opponent can make a two-way hook that scores big points.

Here's what I mean:

If I play the word TUMOR to start the game and I place the T on the double-letter square, I will score 16 points.

Say my opponent can then play HEM, HO, and ER for 26 points.

If, instead, I place TUMOR so that the O goes on the center starred double-word-score space, I get only 14 points, but when my opponent then plays HEM, HO and ER, she can score only 15 points.

Try not to put a vowel next to a hot spot!

Let's see how this works in practice with some quiz problems.

QUIZ FOUR: TWO-WAY PLAYS

Q1. Your opponent goes first and plays FINER with the F on a double letter score for 24 points. Your rack is
A A E N P R W
What's your best play?

Q2. Same situation as #1, but your rack is
C G H O L R U

Q3. Same situation; your rack is
A E F L I M O

Q4. You started with FINER, and your opponent played the best response to #3. Your rack:
D E E E I N R

Q5. You opponent started the game by playing HIP with the I in the middle star square. You have
A B O O Q T U

Q6. Your opponent starts the game with BOTH with the O in the middle star square. Your rack:
A E E I M N X

For answers, see page 52.

CHAPTER 18
Expanding Your Scrabble Vocabulary

EMPLOYING THE BINGO STRATEGY, LOOKING for hot spots and two-way hooks, and working to improve your anagramming ability are all key skills. If you work on these skills, your game will improve tremendously even if you don't expand your knowledge of acceptable Scrabble words. If you want to make further strides, however, consider working on your Scrabble vocabulary.

Remember that a Scrabble vocabulary is not the same as a normal working vocabulary in English. A robust everyday vocabulary is, of course, an asset; you will spot words that an opponent with a limited vocabulary will miss—but not as many of them as someone who has a good Scrabble vocabulary.

If you start using a lot of Scrabble words in your play, your casual opponents may start asking you what those words mean. Some may even object to your playing words that you can't define. There's nothing wrong with learning definitions, of course, and the *Official Scrabble Players Dictionary* has short definitions for every word. But there is nothing in the Scrabble rules that says you have to know definitions in order to play the words.

Vocabulary I

There are two basic levels of Scrabble vocabulary expansion. This is the method I've used most of my life (since I don't compete at the tournament level):

Learn your two-letter words. If you do not learn the "Twos," you are going to be severely handicapped.

Learn other words by playing a lot of Scrabble games, preferably against better opponents. The more games you play, the more words you will pick up.

This is all you really have to do. Keep playing, and you will learn more words.

Vocabulary II

If, however, you want to improve your game much faster, get and study the "Cheat Sheet." It's a handy resource that can be downloaded from cross-tables.com/cs. (Note there is one for "home and school players" that does not include the banned words; I recommend using the "tournament" players list.)

Here's a quick look at what's on the Cheat Sheet and how to work with it:

Two-letter words.

Three-letter words. Obviously most people cannot memorize this long a list. But learning as many "threes" as possible will really help your game, especially since many of them are "hooks" onto the "twos."

I started, as you can, by taking the list and eliminating all the common words you already know. Then, as you play more games, you will learn more three-letter words as a matter of course and start coming up with ways to memorize them. For instance, I know that *am* will take three vowels after it to make the words *ama, ami, amu*—as well as a *p* to make *amp*.

Eventually you will whittle the list down to fewer than 200 words you need to memorize, and, if you keep at it, you will know 90 or 95 percent of the "Threes" and you can keep striving for absolute perfection.

Words with J, Q, X, and Z. The Cheat Sheet provides four handy lists of words of four letters or less that contain the powerful high-scoring tiles J, Q, X, and Z. It really pays off to learn these words (many of them you will pick up by playing). I think the J and Z words are particularly worth studying, because there is a higher percentage of them that are unfamiliar.

Vowel dumps. On the second page of the Cheat Sheet are some handy lists of words that will help you to fix your unbalanced racks by getting rid of several vowels without using more than one consonant. Playing these words will help you balance your rack and get you some points instead of having to trade in letters. The separate lists of I Dumps and U Dumps allow you to play two of those duplicate vowels in one short word. Learning these is helpful, and remember: because *qi* is now an acceptable word, you no longer should worry about keeping a U in your rack so you don't get stuck with the Q at the end of the game. Getting stuck with the Q is now a rare occurrence.

Also on the Cheat Sheet is a list of all the letters that hook onto the beginning and end of all the two-letter words—a very good thing to know.

In addition, there's a section that tells you all the bingos that can be made by adding any letter to the most productive "bingo stems" of six-letter racks: TISANE, SATIRE, and RETAIN.

Many more lists of bingo stems and other helpful resources can be found online; see the Appendix for a list of some of those resources.

CHAPTER 19
Bluffing and Challenging

THERE'S ANOTHER RULE YOU MUST be aware of: the rule on challenging.

If your opponent plays a word you doubt, you can challenge it. The word is looked up in your agreed-upon official dictionary. If the word is no good, your opponent takes it off the board and loses a turn. However, if the word is correct and your challenge fails, then you lose your turn.

This rule means that you can sometimes get away with bluffing, if your opponent decides not to challenge.

It's not a good idea to deliberately play phony words. Not only is it a losing strategy against good players, it won't endear you to your opponents if you do it too frequently.

But there are times when bluffing is perhaps your only hope, or when you decide it's worth the risk. In this case, here are some rough guidelines to follow:

Play a word that is plausible. In many cases, you might play a word you think (or hope) is a bingo, a word that sounds like or is spelled similarly to a word you know is good, or a word that follows the rules of English word formation.

You are much more likely to succeed in playing something like MINATION than in playing INNAMOTI—even though neither word is good, the former at least sounds like it *might* be a real English word.

Play swiftly and confidently. Don't openly express doubts about a word you are playing!

Whether or not *you* choose to bluff, your opponent may sometimes play a word you suspect is not in the official dictionary. She may

43

do so intentionally as a deliberate phony, or the play may be made unintentionally (a misspelling or a word she thinks is good).

Note: When you challenge, you automatically have the right to challenge each word made on your opponent's play. If any of them are wrong, you win the challenge.

Challenging a word involves a big risk. You will lose your turn if the word is good. So when is it right to challenge?

You should weigh several factors:

1. Your own word knowledge. *How certain are you that this word is wrong?* If you absolutely know the word is bad, you should challenge it. But you should be quite certain—there are many allowable words in the Scrabble dictionary that I'm quite sure you don't know.

2. Your knowledge of your opponent. *How good is your opponent? How often does she play phonies?* If your opponent is a very good player and knows lots of words you don't, challenging becomes more difficult. If you know that your opponent often plays phonies, you should be more willing to call her bluff. If you know your opponent *never* plays phonies, then don't challenge.

3. Your opportunities. *Does the phony word create a great scoring chance for you?* If you're considering a challenge, say "stop" and take a moment to look at the opportunities the word has created for you. If it opens up a spot for you to play a bingo or a high-scoring non-bingo, then factor in the value of your next play with the value of your opponent's play. Sometimes you are better off accepting a word you know is wrong!

4. The value of the word played. *Is it a game-breaker or just a nuisance?* If the suspect word is a bingo or another high-scoring play, then the stakes are high. If it's just a low-scoring play, ask yourself if it is really worth the risk of challenging it.

5. The game score and situation. *Is it worth the risk at this point in the game?* Calculate the consequences of your challenge on your goal of winning the game. If you're comfortably ahead late in the game, you should be less likely to challenge and potentially give your opponent an extra turn to catch up. If you're behind late in the game, however, the challenge may be your only hope. If your opponent's word ends the game, you should *always* challenge because there's absolutely no risk!

Earlier in the game, the choice becomes less clear. You don't want to risk squandering a lead *or* blowing your chance to get back in a game you're losing. But weigh carefully what the score will become if you don't challenge, if you challenge successfully, and if you challenge unsuccessfully.

Also, if your opponent plays a bingo you don't know with a blank and other good bingo tiles, you should consider that she is likely to get another bingo soon anyway. You might be less likely to challenge in this situation.

Everything in this section also applies to your decision whether or not to try to play a phony word: your knowledge of your opponent, the value of your phony, and the game stage and score.

Let's do an exercise about this.

QUIZ FIVE: CHALLENGING

For each item, mark YES if you would challenge, NO if you would not challenge. Do NOT consult the dictionary! Answers are on page 53.

Q1. Your opponent opens the game by playing ANTINGS, with a blank for one of the Ns.

Q2. You are ahead by 50 points late in the game and your opponent plays JUKU, JO, UT, KA, and UR for 32 points.

Q3. You are behind by 30 points in the middle of the game and your opponent plays OUTCOOKS for 83 points, opening up a spot for you to make a 70-point bingo.

Q4. You are ahead by 20 points in the middle of the game and your opponent, known for making phonies, plays OTALGIA for 68 points.

Q5. You are behind by 104 points at the end of the game. Your opponent, who has never played a phony against you, plays VUV for 12 points.

Q6. Same as #5, but you are ahead by 80 points.

Q7. Your opponent goes out playing FUBAR for 21 points, enough to surpass your score and win by 2.

Q8. Your opponent plays GOOGLED to pull within 40 points of you. She pulls the last four letters from the bag. Both blanks have been played.

Q9. The score is virtually tied in the middle of the game. A well-known bluffer plays WUD and WAB on the same turn for 36 points.

Q10. With 10 tiles left in the pool, you are winning by 90 points. Your opponent plays MGATHM for 35 points.

Q11. Your opponent is behind by 20 late in the game and plays CWM. The play leaves you two points ahead

CHAPTER 20
The End Game

IF YOU ARE IN A close game and the letters are dwindling, you have a huge advantage if you know what letters are in your opponent's rack. Then you can play an intelligent "end game" that might involve blocking places to keep your opponent from going out first or from making a decisive high-scoring play.

There are score sheets you can get that enable you to count the letters as they are played. Or you can do so yourself on a sheet of paper. If you do this, make sure you don't miss a turn, or you will lose track of what's been played.

I use a different strategy. If the game is close and there are only a few tiles left in the bag, I take a few minutes and mark off the letters that are played on the board, row by row from the top. Then I add the tiles that are in my rack, and I have a precise count of what letters remain. At the end of the game I know exactly what tiles are in my opponent's rack.

The nuances of the end game are beyond the scope of this book, but between two good players it can be like a chess match: trying to figure out how to stop your opponent from scoring big or going out while trying to make your best scoring plays. You're at a big disadvantage if you don't know the letters your opponent has.

At the very least, you should make sure you know whether either blank, any of the four Ss, or any of the four high-scoring tiles remain unplayed If you have time, you should also scan for the K, and the missing four- and three-point tiles. Most game boards have the list of tiles and their frequencies printed on them to help you—or refer back to Chapter 5.

CHAPTER 21
Make Your Own Luck

IF YOU FOLLOW THE ADVICE in this book, you will definitely improve your game.

Keep practicing. Scrabble will become much more challenging and much more fun as you go along.

The key intangible is to approach your game with confidence. I firmly believe you help to make your own luck. If you are negative and concentrate on defense and avoiding mistakes, you will lose more often than win. But if you play aggressively and look for opportunities, they will present themselves. Some games you'll be unlucky, but in the long run you'll control your fate.

APPENDIX
Resources

The North American Scrabble Players Association. Get all the information needed at www.scrabbleplayers.org. Fees are small and include a valuable newsletter.

Cross-tables.com. A guide to competitive Scrabble that includes the valuable Cheat Sheet plus information about tournaments and much more.

The Seattle Scrabble club website has a tremendous collection of sources—word lists, books, basics—at www.seattlescrabble.org/study.php.

Another source for word lists is Joyce's Scrabble Mania at www.geocities.com/~rosella/scrabbble/wordlist.html.

The official Scrabble score sheet that's used in tournaments, and can help you keep track of the letters played, is at scrabble-assoc.com/forms/scoresheet.pdf.

Game boards, tiles, racks, and other products can be found at www.adjudicator3000.com.

Protiles—the tiles the experts use—can be obtained at www.protiles.net. One big advantage of Protiles is that replacements for lost tiles are free.

There are additional resources on the web.

QUIZ ANSWERS

Answers to Quiz One are in Chapter 7.

QUIZ TWO: INITIAL PLAY

1. A A E G M N T   Play MAGENTA for a bingo.

2. B C M P V W Y   Trade in all your letters.

3. D R S S T U *   Play TRUSSED for 66 points.

4. D D R S S U *   Keep the blank and an S and trade in the rest.

5. D N O S U Y Z   Play ZOUNDS for 52 points.

6. A E F G H H I   Play HIGH for 22 points. The letters you leave, A E F, aren't terrible.

7. A B C E S V V   CAVES gets you 26 points, but loses your S and leaves you B, V. Instead, consider trading all but the S.

8. D O O O O O V   Play VOODOO for 28 points.

QUIZ THREE: SECOND PLAY OF THE GAME

WORD ON BOARD	YOUR TILES	YOUR PLAY

1. GIMP**S**   D G I O Q T U Play QUOIT, QI, UM, OP, and IS all on one turn!

2. RAT**E**   A E I I N R T Play INERTIA and IRATE.

3. B**O**X   C C G I I N O Play ICONIC and XI.

4. **TO**ILING   A E M N O R V Play MANGROVE.

5. LA**DY**   N O P S S S * Play SYNOPSIS.

6. KUDO**S**   C E I I R S T Play STICKIER.

7. UN**FIT**   B C E R O U X Play CRUX or ROUX and XU.

8. NEW**T**   E F G I O R * Play FORGIVEN or FORGIVES, NE, and ES.

QUIZ FOUR: TWO-WAY PLAYS

Q1. Play PAW, PI, AN, and WE for 27 points.

Q2. Play HOG, HE, and OR for 24 points.

Q3. Play LIFER, LI, IN, FE, and ER for 28 points.

Q4. With LIFER and FINER on the board, play NEEDIER, INN, FEE, and ERE and chalk up 74 points.

Q5. Play QUOTA, QI, and UP for 31 points.

Q6. Play EXAMINE, BE, OX, TI, and HM for 93 points.

QUIZ FIVE: CHALLENGING

1. NO. She's got good bingo letters, so leave it be (even if it turns out to be a phony).

2. YES. You have learned your two-letter words—you know UR isn't good.

3. NO. You are happy with your bingo.

4. NO. You're still in the game, so don't get further behind by challenging a good word.

5. YES. Your cause is hopeless if you don't challenge.

6. NO. If you're not sure VUV is bad, don't risk it—you're ahead.

7. YES because otherwise you lose (though you lose anyway because FUBAR is good).

8. NO because you should be able to keep your lead.

9. NO. The words are good. Know your three-letter words.

10. YES. Doesn't sound like an English word, does it?

11. NO. The score is still close—and you might know the word is good.